ASSESSMENT thAT WORKs

ASSESSMENT thAT WORKs

How do you know how much they know?
A guide to asking the right questions

John Sleigh

Copyright © 2018 by John Sleigh.

ISBN: Softcover   978-1-9845-0132-5
        eBook   978-1-9845-0131-8

All rights reserved. No part of this book may be reproduced or transmitted in any form or by any means, electronic or mechanical, including photocopying, recording, or by any information storage and retrieval system, without permission in writing from the copyright owner.

Print information available on the last page.

Rev. date: 08/07/2018

To order additional copies of this book, contact:
Xlibris
1-800-455-039
www.Xlibris.com.au
Orders@Xlibris.com.au
781802

CONTENTS

Competency based assessment 1
    Describing Knowledge 1
THE PURPOSE 7
    Your target 7
THE PRINCIPLES 14
    Is the process fair? 14
    Is the assessment flexible? 22
    Is the assessment valid? 25
    Is the result reliable? 28
    Does it match the level? 29
    Ethics 31
    Legislation 32
    Organisation and industry standards 34
THE CONTEXT 37
    National Competency Standards 37
DESIGN 44
    Content 45
EVIDENCE 46
    Sufficient 46
    Authentic 48
    Current 50
MAPPING THE ASSESSMENT TO A COMPETENCY 51
SAMPLES 56
    Paired choice 56
    Matched Choice 57
    Multiple Choice 59
    Induction programs 63
    Question layout 67
    Practical Demonstrations 86
    Log books 92

*Dedicated to my son Griffin
for his innate ability to ask the right question.*

COMPETENCY BASED ASSESSMENT

Assessment at work can be used to confirm ability to do the job. It is also useful as a selection technique, for transfer, reassignment or promotion or to confirm the effect of training, perhaps with transfer, reassignment or promotion in mind. In an era where the world is changing rapidly, professionals are expected to prove that have maintained their competency. Lawyers, doctors, accountants, surveyors, school teachers, cab drivers and coal miners all need to show that they have added to their knowledge through continuous professional development.

Assessment tasks may include

1. Simulate a decision that the candidate may have to make;
2. Ask a candidate to do a task they would be expected to do on the job
3. Prepare a report
4. Interpret a report prepared by others
5. Check if the candidate remembers essential information covered during the training;

Assessment that works is mostly concerned with the skills and knowledge necessary to do a job.

Describing Knowledge

In 1956, Benjamin Bloom defined a "Taxonomy of Educational Objectives for the Cognitive Domain."

In this discussion we will refer to what are often called "levels" as "objectives." We will use the word "level" to refer to the Australian

Quality Training Framework (AQTF) competency levels. The AQTF is explained on pages 29 to 31.

Bloom listed 6 objectives for a learning program:

- Knowledge
- Comprehension
- Application
- Analysis
- Synthesis
- Evaluation.

For adult learning, a case can be made for a lower grade objective of awareness. I will not make that case in detail here but will occasionally refer to awareness as an objective at a lower standard than "recall."

I also prefer the synonyms "recall" for "knowledge" and "understanding" for "comprehension" when discussing adult learning in this context. I find the word "knowledge" is useful to cover all the objectives. Throughout this book I have tried to choose the simplest word available if it didn't confuse the issue. To me understanding is a simpler way of saying comprehension.

Competency based training is targeted at the awareness, knowledge, understanding and application steps of Bloom's taxonomy.

An entry level employee would be expected to meet awareness and recall objectives. An experienced employee would use awareness, recall and understanding to apply what they have learned. A problem solver or supervisor would also analyse the learning, as well as meeting the earlier objectives. The higher levels, synthesis and evaluation usually have higher order use.

For the purposes of this book and its application to assessment in the workplace, here is what I mean by my adaptation of Bloom's terms:

Awareness. A great deal of work activity may not need detailed knowledge, but merely recognise that something is present, absent or changing. A customer service specialist needs to be aware of the customer's mood to give useful service. A school bus driver needs to aware of the noises heard both from the back seats and the engine. This is not as detailed as "knowledge", from Bloom's list or "recall" from my adaptation.

1. Are these statements true or false?

   a) *All people learn the same way.*
   b) *Experience is a great teacher.*
   c) *Everyone could get a perfect score in a test if they were given enough time.*
   d) *A single picture explains more clearly than a thousand words.*

Throughout the book there are sequentially numbered examples of assessment questions related to the nearby content.

Recall means knowing precise details. Price for the salesperson, speed limits and passenger numbers for the school bus driver. Much of an entry level employee's work will be about reaching target numbers or checking that standards are being maintained. To do either they need to know what those targets or standards are.

2. Name the objectives in Bloom's taxonomy.

As well as naming, the questions might ask to "define, describe, identify, list or match."

Understanding goes deeper. Apart from knowing what the right value should be, the person who understands will recognise the things that led to that value being reached and those that prevent it being maintained. Meeting a customer's need, where they are not sure exactly what they want also requires understanding of what alternatives are available and what solutions are offered.

3. Select the appropriate product from our range for a customer who is looking for …

Add your own ending. Apart from selecting from a list, to assess understanding you might like to start the question with "explain, estimate, rewrite, distinguish," or perhaps ask them to "defend" a position or proposition.

Application means using the information to achieve a goal. This is more than answering a question or making a choice. Experienced employees are expected to apply their knowledge when circumstances change. This is a large part of a supervisor's role. A technician may also spend much of the work day in this mode. It is about converting abstract concepts into concrete action.

I haven't given any specific example of questions for this and the following objectives, as the number of questions is as wide as the number of jobs. Most jobs are to apply. Most workplace training is targeted at teaching application. The terms that start the question include "operate, demonstrate, change, use and show." The activities associated with apply could include "lift, separate, join, build or enter details."

Analysis involves dividing an issue into contributing parts. A job that includes fault finding or problem solving will require analysis. For marketers, the question is "if this variable changes, what will happen then?" This is also the basis of scientific discovery. It also provides the basis for two eminent lawyers arguing passionately and convincingly in court. The objective may be to "compare, distinguish, outline or subdivide." Activities might include "interpret, translate, categorise, examine or explore."

Synthesis combines knowledge from various sources. Creative roles such as advertising or journalism rely on synthesis. University written assignments are based on supporting or demolishing an argument based on cited references. This is synthesis. I have taken the work of Kirkpatrick and Bloom and blended in the standards of the AQF and my knowledge of mining to put forward a formula for designing assessments. The objectives may begin with "compile, compose, create, design or construct." The activities may include "combine, develop, formulate or derive." Often analysis is about investigating a past event, while synthesis is about forecasting.

Evaluation involves judgement rather than just knowledge. Judges from the wine show all the way to the courthouse evaluate. They consider available information and "appraise, compare or criticise." A scientific hypothesis is based on evaluation of previous work. The marketing plan for a new product launch also relied heavily on evaluation of many factors. Apart from judging, evaluation activities could include "optimise, adjudicate, rank or classify."

The target is to reach a standard that has been established. In Bloom terms, it deals with recall or understanding of a set amount of knowledge and the application of defined skills. It is not an education program searching for new information through analysis of existing material or experimentation in new fields. The value of competency in the workplace is to maintain a defined quality. This does discredit the value of research or experimentation, just defines the boundaries within which most of the workforce will operate.

But why another book?

My reason for writing this book stems from a dissatisfaction with the standard of assessment questions that I have found in the mining industry. I have no reason to believe that it is any better or worse in other industries. Many of the examples used in this book are based on a very unlikely subject – coal mining under Queensland law. There are two advantages, one it is a subject I know well, so I can see nuances. Two, it is a subject that I expect you will know little about, so you will be able to focus on the construction of the question rather than the accuracy of the answer. You can then take that construction and apply it to a subject you do know the answer to.

I also refer to the Australian Quality Training Framework competencies for workplace trainers and assessors. Like mining, assessment has its own language. I have tried to use the terms that are used in this valuable, benchmark skillset.

For those who are not miners, you might like to replicate this next activity for your industry to show how no matter where we work we speak a language that is foreign to those from outside the industry.

4. Do you know what these words mean?

Rib, Face, Bottoms, Isolation, Chain, Heading, Brush, Creep, Borer, Tube, Gate, Shield, Chock, Outburst, Door, Fall, Shot, Blower, Overcast, Grade, Anchor, Plate.

In mining each has a different meaning to what you may be used to.

I trust that you will be able to translate the techniques offered in this book to your location and needs.

You may like to experiment with the words for snow if you are an Eskimo, or perhaps play with the differences in the meaning of these words:

5. Place these words in the order of relevance to your objectives:

Education, training, school, teaching, evaluation, assessment, examination, testing, instruction, pedagogy, andragogy, curriculum, qualification, competence, didactic, coaching, mentoring, lecture, lesson, refresher, facilitate, inform, knowledge, understanding, application, awareness, class, study, syllabus, inculcation, upbringing, induction, orientation, faculty, pupil, student, trainee, apprentice, impart, seminar, professor, graduate, instil, academy.

Alternatively:

6. Select 10 words from the list in Question 5 that apply to your assessment activity.

Competency based assessment is about topics that affect the ability of a person to perform a task. An automotive mechanic needs to be aware of the dangers of exhaust fumes so that a car is not left running in an unventilated workshop.

If your assessment is competency based, then your target audience will have different needs to one where the objective is research.

THE PURPOSE

Dr. Donald Kirkpatrick (1924 – 2014) described four purposes for assessment, Reaction, Learning, Behaviour and Results. His 1954 PhD thesis, 1959 articles for the American Society of Training and Development and a book published in 1994 are among the milestones of his lifetime of work on the subject, and like Bloom's work in the same era his targets remain important today. These questions about Kirkpatrick's model show different ways of asking the same question to relate to the different purposes. While it is unlikely that a student at less than certificate 4 would be expected to know this material, the questions are set using his principles to show ways that the same question can be asked for different target audiences.

Kirkpatrick's model is often referred to as levels of assessment. In this book, because we are also using levels to describe the level of competence under the AQTF guideline, I have used the word "purpose" to describe Kirkpatrick's terms.

Your target

Questions 7 and 8 are suitable for Certificate 2 assessments. The student is expected to remember common terms or to match the term with its meaning. At certificate 2 or 3 they would not be expected to remember the exact wording of the definition. They could be expected to remember the simpler descriptions used in the second example in question 8.

7. Name Kirkpatrick's four purposes for assessment

You may ask for them in order or be satisfied with a list.

- Behaviour
- Learning
- Reaction
- Results

8. Match Kirkpatrick's definition with the purpose:

Behaviour		The degree to which participants acquire the intended knowledge, skills, attitude, confidence and commitment based on their participation in the training
Learning		The degree to which participants apply what they learned during training when they are back on the job
Reaction		The degree to which participants find the training favourable, engaging and relevant to their jobs
Results		The degree to which targeted outcomes occur as a result of the training and the support and accountability package

You may choose to use the formal definition from Kirkpatrick's work, or these simple descriptions

Behaviour		Can you do it?
Learning		Do you do it?
Reaction		Does it make a difference?
Results		Was it interesting?

Question 7 could be suitable for certificate 2 if either the names of the purposes or the definitions are provided. Otherwise it would be at least certificate 3 level.

9. Define Kirkpatrick's four purposes for assessment

You may list the name of the purpose or ask them to. The order that they are set out in these questions is not Kirkpatrick's order. This will reduce successful guessing

Behaviour	*The degree to which participants acquire the intended knowledge, skills, attitude, confidence and commitment based on their participation in the training*
Learning	*The degree to which participants apply what they learned during training when they are back on the job*
Reaction	*The degree to which participants find the training favourable, engaging and relevant to their jobs*
Results	*The degree to which targeted outcomes occur as a result of the training and the support and accountability package*

This asks the student to interpret the definition, which they are expected to remember. A question as complex as this is suitable for Certificate 4 and above. Question 8 could be made less complex if the four purposes were named, for example, if you ask "Which purpose describes each action, Reaction, Learning, Behaviour or Results?

The next question matches the certificate level with the description:

10. Which of Kirkpatrick's purposes of assessment match each description or question?

You may name the purpose or ask them to. In this example there are more questions than purposes.

  a) *Did the students think the venue was comfortable?*

b) The students completed a pre-training assessment.
c) The students pre-training survey was compared with the after-course assessment
d) Did the students think the lesson was relevant to their job?
e) Are the skills developed in training being used by the students who do the training?
f) Has there been a reduction in costs since the employees were trained?
g) Did the students take part in the activities?
h) Has the accident rate has reduced since the training?
i) Can the students answer questions about the subject?

Question 11 allows you to evaluate your assessment against Kirkpatrick's guidance.

11. Which purpose is your assessment question addressing?

a) Do you think that Kirkpatrick's model suits your assessment strategy?
b) Can you give examples of each of the purposes in the model?
c) Will you now set questions that address each purpose?
d) Which purpose is most effectively met in your case?

Reaction

When you design questions to measure audience feedback, avoid creating a smile sheet. I have found these questions a useful way to gain and use participant feedback.

12. What surprising information did you hear for the first time today?

This question encourages them to list what they gained from the session. If the answer is "nothing," accept it and target your material to their needs next time. But I have never had a blank response to that question.

This is particularly valuable for refresher training programs. Where the people are attending programs to maintain their competency, the content will include both information they have forgotten and information that has changed since the earlier times they attended. Answers to this question can reassure you that you are providing relevant material.

13. What did we discuss today that you will use first when you go back to work?

This doesn't look for information that must be new, just something that was useful.

14. What will you tell your best friend you did today?

You will be amazed at the range of answers that you will get to that question.

Learning

Most of the suggested assessment questions and activities in this book deal with learning or knowledge. Assessment during the program and at the end can measure learning. **Formative Assessment** is done during the program, perhaps after an activity or at the completion of a topic. It may look at the material just covered, or the content that will be dealt with next. **Summative Assessment** is the assessment at the completion of the seminar or after a brief period back on the job.

15. What do you know about Formative Assessment?

A question like this can provide a good formative assessment activity. Leave space in the workbook for them to write their notes. Then turn it into a group activity. Provide a different coloured pen and ask them to add to their notes through a group discussion.

Photograph the workbook pages so that you have a record of what each individual knew, and what each thought was important from the group activity.

I have found that designing workbooks so that key pages can be scanned or photographed can provide a measure of what was gained through group discussion.

Behaviour

The objective of most training is a change in behaviour in the workplace. Summative assessment measures the knowledge at the end of the session. Questions 12, 13 and 14 measure reaction, but as so often happens they have a secondary purpose, too. Question 13 and, to a lesser extent, questions 12 and 14 also measure learning and intended behaviour.

Kirkpatrick saw the measurement of actual behaviour as equally valuable.

16. Rank the value of these measures of behaviour after training.

   a) ___Survey of the supervisor
   b) ___Survey of the student, one week later
   c) ___Survey of the student one month later
   d) ___Survey of the student one year later
   e) ___Measure of a relevant Key Performance Indicator
   f) ___Follow up questions asked by the student
   g) ___Observation on the job
   h) ___Observations of quality of product or service after the training

The periods mentioned in options (b), (c) and (d) can be applied to the other options.

Results

Kirkpatrick's fourth measure of assessment was "Does it make any difference?"

Between 1990 and 1994 Australian employers who had a total payroll above $200,000 had to pay 1.5% of their payroll to the government as a training guarantee levy. The amount spent on training by the employer were credited as exemptions from the levy.

17. Which of these do you believe occurred during the period that the Training Guarantee levy was in force?

   a) *An employer with several separate stores registered each of the stores as a separate company, so that the payroll for each entity was the minimum. For example, instead of one company owning six stores with a total payroll of $900,000, and a levy obligation of $13,500, each of the stores stayed under the $200,000 threshold, so had no levy obligation.*
   b) *An organisation which had an annual training budget which equalled 2.2% of their payroll reduced their training budget to the levy amount, 1.5%.*
   c) *Executive teams held their training and development activities in overseas resorts and charged the cost against the levy.*

Regrettably all happened.

Another feared result of training is that we will pay to train our people and they will leave. If that worries you, then think about the results if you do not train your people and they stay.

THE PRINCIPLES

Competency based assessments must be:

- Fair
- Flexible
- Valid
- Reliable

And the evidence must be

- Sufficient
- Authentic, and
- Current.

In addition to these principles of assessment there are ethical and legal standards that an assessor must meet.

Is the process fair?

Are the needs of the learner considered in the assessment process?

The assessment task should not need a higher level of knowledge, literacy, numeracy or physical skill than they need to carry out the job they are training for.

If the candidate has the necessary knowledge before training, they may meet the requirements for Recognition of Prior Learning (RPL). A pre-training assessment can also set the standard at which the training will be delivered. If a student already knows most of what is covered in the training, they are likely to be distracted when other, unknown contest is introduced. Current knowledge can also be assessed and reinforced through class discussions. These can be led early in the session or as more complex material is introduced.

Literacy

The language used in an assessment should be at the same level as that needed on the job.

The Australian Skills Quality Authority (ASQA) sets the standard for assessment for Australian Registered Training Organisations (RTOs). They require assessments to be fair, flexible, reliable and valid.

Together, these mean that the skills being assessed test the ability of the person to do the work.

There is a reading level calculator built into many spelling and grammar checkers. The tool in Microsoft Word calculates the Flesch Reading Ease on a scale of 0 to 100%. The higher scores are easier to read. It also calculates the number of years of school education that a reader would need to understand the text clearly.

This statement is taken from the ASQA's standard for RTOs. It explains one of the requirements for assessment.

> *Validity requires:*
>
> a. *assessment against the unit(s) of competency and the associated assessment requirements covers the broad range of skills and knowledge that are essential to competent performance;*
> b. *assessment of knowledge and skills is integrated with their practical application;*
> c. *assessment to be based on evidence that demonstrates that a learner could demonstrate these skills and knowledge in other similar situations; and*
> d) *judgement of competence is based on evidence of learner performance that is aligned to the unit/s of competency and associated assessment requirements.*

Now compare this explanation of validity, written for this guide:

> *A unit of competency sets out the skills and knowledge that is needed to do a part of a job. A valid assessment is one which uses the standards needed to do the job. A weight that has be lifted in the assessment should be about the same as a weight lifted on the job. Any lifting equipment available on the job, should be used in the assessment. Not every step has to be tested. A skill or knowledge in one area may apply in other areas, too.*
>
> *The words used in an assessment task should be at the same level as the language used on the job. If an English speaking person must do the work, it is fair to carry out the assessment in English.*

18. Can you pick which paragraph matches each of these readability standards?

    a) *Lower average number of words per sentence?*
    b) *Lower average number of syllables per word?*
    c) *Would be suitable for a person who has had 7 years education?*
    d) *Would suit a person who has had 14 years education?*

19. List the points that were made in one paragraph that were not made in the other.

Or, to place the assessment at Certificate 2 level:

20. Which of these points was only made in one of the paragraphs? There may be more than one.

    a) *A valid assessment tests the skills and knowledge needed to do the job*
    b) *Testing of knowledge and skills can be done on the job*
    c) *An assessment can be done in a simulated work environment*
    d) *The skills and knowledge to be tested are set out in the Unit of Competency.*

Reading ease

The reading ease is affected by:

- The number of characters in a word;
- The number of syllables in a word;
- The number of words in a sentence;
- The number of sentences in a paragraph.

Fitness

An assessment should not require a higher level of fitness than is needed to do the job. Mining legislation states that no person may go underground unless they are capable of "self-escape." This means a lot of things, one of which is able to walk from their workplace to the surface if there is an emergency. There is also a requirement that from time to time people who work underground take part in an emergency evacuation. This means that it is a reasonable requirement that anyone working underground be able to walk 10 km under stressful conditions.

It is equally fair to expect a person to be able to evacuate down stairs from a high rise building if they work in the upper levels. If they have a phobia about heights or elevators or a physical or psychological condition that prevents them going above the first floor, it is not fair to include the ability to escape from the top floor if they work on the ground floor.

Knowledge of legislation

We are all expected to abide by the law. Ignorance of the law is no excuse. But that may not mean that we have to know the precise details of the legislation. It is quite possible to drive a car, stay under the speed limits, overtake safely and park legally in a foreign country, without learning a copy of their legislation. Signs and standards are very similar, and there are one page summaries of the differences available from travel agents.

I found this question in an induction program for new starters in the industry:

21. Section 39 of the Coal Mining Safety and Health Act, 1999 sets out the obligations of persons generally

TRUE / FALSE. These are the obligations of all people on the mine property:

(1) A coal mine worker or other person at a coal mine or a person who may affect the safety and health of others at a coal mine or as a result of coal mining operations has the following obligations—

   (a) to comply with this Act and procedures applying to the worker or person that are part of a safety and health management system for the mine;
   (b) if the coal mine worker or other person has information that other persons need to know to fulfil their obligations or duties under this Act, or to protect themselves from the risk of injury or illness, to give the information to the other persons;
   (c) to take any other reasonable and necessary course of action to ensure anyone is not exposed to an unacceptable level of risk.

(2) A coal mine worker or other person at a coal mine has the following additional obligations—

   (a) to work or carry out the worker's or person's activities in a way that does not expose the worker or person or someone else to an unacceptable level of risk;
   (b) to ensure, to the extent of the responsibilities and duties allocated to the worker or person, that the work and activities under the worker's or person's control, supervision, or leadership is conducted in a way that does not expose the worker or person or someone else to an unacceptable level of risk;
   (c) to the extent of the worker's or person's involvement, to participate in and conform to the risk management practices of the mine;

(d) to comply with instructions given for safety and health of persons by the coal mine operator or site senior executive for the mine or a supervisor at the mine;
(e) to work at the coal mine only if the worker or person is in a fit condition to carry out the work without affecting the safety and health of others;
(f) not to do anything wilfully or recklessly that might adversely affect the safety and health of someone else at the mine.

I am not sure what the assessors found out about the candidates from that question.

There is a significant difference between recall of the wording of legislation, or policy, and its application. I cannot imagine a case where the intent of legislation or policy was not its ultimate application.

Generally, a competency standard will not say that you must be able to quote legislation. It may say that you must interpret, access or follow. Here are some ways that knowledge of the underlying requirements of that legislation could be assessed.

22. What does the Queensland Coal Mining Safety and Health Act, Section 39, specifically say about communicating information and receiving instructions?

To answer this question, you need to know what section 39 of the Act says. There will be many experienced, competent miners who know that they have the obligations referred to, but who may not connect them to section 39.

The section deals with the obligations, "if the coal mine worker or other person has information that other persons need to know to fulfil their obligations or duties under this Act, or to protect themselves from the risk of injury or illness, to give the information to the other persons;" and "to comply with instructions given for safety and health of persons by the coal mine operator or site senior executive for the mine or a supervisor at the mine."

The competency asks you to access, identify, interpret, follow and apply, not state, recite or remember. It is usually about documents, procedures, standards, not Acts or Regulations. The person preparing the document or procedure makes sure it complies. The person doing the job is asked to follow the instructions developed by others. This is almost always the case for level 2 and 3, and often for level 4 or 5.

It may say something like:

RIIRIS201D
1.1 Access, interpret and apply risk management documentation and ensure the work activity is compliant

RIIERR203D:
1.1 Access, interpret and apply emergency response and rescue documentation and ensure the work activity is compliant

RIIGOV201D:
2.1 Carry out allocated work to procedures/standards

RIICOM201D:
1.1 Access, interpret and apply communication site documentation and ensure the work activity is compliant

RIIERR302D:
2.1 Identify, confirm and follow emergency evacuation procedures

RIIRIS402D:
1.1 Access, interpret and apply risk management documentation and ensure the work activity is compliant

Testing memory

There are some things that a competent person must remember. For example, an office worker would be expected to answer the phone in a particular way.

You may expect more than one short answer to the same question. You may decide that competent candidates may only be able to remember part of a list of alternatives.

23. Where would you expect to find a telephone if you were working underground in a conveyor belt roadway?

There are at least 9 possible, correct answers in section 176 of the Coal Mining Safety and Health Regulation, 2017. For a level 2 or level 3 assessment, you may only expect 3 or 4 answers, although any of the nine are correct.

Expected answers

- In the crib room
- Near the drivehead
- Near the transformer
- Near the transfer point
- At the face

Possible answers

- each entrance underground, and on the surface, through which a person may enter into a shaft or other excavation used for ingress to or egress from the mine workings;
- each underground battery charging station;
- each underground workshop;
- each underground crib room;
- a place close to each switchgear used to isolate or control sections of the underground main electricity distribution system; (transformer or isolator)
- a place close to each underground conveyor belt drivehead;
- a place close to each underground loading or transfer point on the conveyor belt system;
- each emergency refuge chamber;

- a place in each inspection district not already mentioned in this list.

Is the assessment flexible?

Adults learn in a variety of ways. The assessment process is not about how we learn, but what we learn.

There is a mnemonic used in many Australian first aid courses, DRSABCD.

It reminds students that the sequence for dealing with a casualty is Danger; Response; Send for help; Airway; Breathing; Circulation; Defibrillation.

The following question does not pass the flexibility test if assessing whether a candidate could effectively manage an unconscious patient:

24. What does DRSABCD stand for?

These questions test that knowledge:

25. A patient appears to have fallen from a ladder. They are holding an electric drill. What would your initial steps be to manage the casualty?

Suitable answers might include:

- Make sure the power is disconnected
- Check that there is no further risk of anything or anyone falling
- Check if the patient is conscious
- Ask any available bystander to call for help and to see if there is a Defibrillator available.
- Provide assisted breathing and cardiac massage.

I wrote that answer by ticking through the words in the memory jogger. But I could have learned the process in many other ways. In fact, when I first learned first aid the prompt was just ABC. But it was emphasised that we should always check for danger to ourselves and further injury to the casualty, check for a response before and after every step of treatment and to ask bystanders to call for help and gather available resources.

26. DRSABCD is a reminder of what to do when you find a casualty that needs first aid treatment. What do the letters stand for?

Defibrillator – Is there one available nearby? Is there anyone I can send to get it who will also be able to set it up? What other first aid equipment is available?

Ring for an ambulance

Safety – Is it safe for me to go to the casualty, can the casualty be safely left where they are?

Assistance – Who is available to help me? How can I call emergency services, if required?

Breathing – Is the patient breathing?

Consciousness – What is the patient's current level? Does the patient have a pulse? What is the rate?

Delegation – Who is available to help me – make phone calls, assist with treatment, keep bystanders away?

Would you mark that answer as correct? Only two of the letters matches the "correct answer." One was in the wrong order. The answer contains all the information. Who would you rather be on the scene when you have an accident, someone who can remember a series of letters or someone who knows what to do, but who doesn't know the acronym?

When designing an assessment, consider the skills and knowledge that are required to perform competently. Do not ask about the training aids that have been used to assist learning.

Dr David Kolb described an adult learning cycle in his 1984 publication "Experiential learning: experience as the source of learning and development."

He said that learning may be the result of

1. Concrete Experience - (a new experience or situation is encountered, or a reinterpretation of existing experience).
2. Reflective Observation of the new experience. (of particular importance are any inconsistencies between experience and understanding).
3. Abstract Conceptualization (reflection gives rise to a new idea, or a modification of an existing abstract concept).
4. Active Experimentation (the learner applies them to the world around them to see what results).

That experiment becomes a new concrete experience and the cycle continues.

The cycle may start at any of the four steps. A lesson may lead to a decision to experiment. An experience may lead to a reflection, which is then compared to knowledge that has been acquired earlier, or perhaps, today, "googled."

The skills and knowledge being assessed in a competency based process should reflect all stages of this adult learning cycle.

27. Explain the four stages of the Adult Learning Cycle

Would be a valid question to check the candidate's knowledge of the theory, the abstract concepts. The question would not meet the flexibility principle of a good assessment, though, as it might require attendance at a lecture where the stages were set out.

28. "Experience is a great teacher" is a common saying. Can you describe other ways that adults can learn, apart from or as well as through experience?

That question could inspire a thoughtful essay from a person who has never heard of the adult learning cycle or Doctor Kolb. Reading a book, or watching a video are equivalent to learning from "abstract concepts." Discussing an experience, or reviewing a report of an incident, with someone else sounds very similar to "reflective observation." Trying different approach by adjusting one or a few elements may be described as "active experimentation."

A flexible assessment strategy would recognise all those answers, and many more.

Is the assessment valid?

Are you checking competency? Look at your assessments and ask yourself,

- "Would a student who had not been trained and had no experience pass the assessment?" Most people should not be able to.
- Would an experienced person who had not done this course pass the assessment? They should be able to.

For example, most people would answer YES to this question:

29. As a plumber, do you have to comply with the Safety and Health Management System at a factory where you are doing repairs? YES / NO

If the aim is to test knowledge, the answer to that question is unlikely to help. On the other hand, on an assessment for plumbers being tested before they are allowed on the factory site, this question tells you what they really know:

30. List 5 things that you would need to know about before starting work on the high-pressure pump line.

Because I am not a plumber I do not know the answer, and you don't need to, unless you are, or unless you employ plumbers.

Would somebody following these rules pass your assessment?

- First, answer only the questions that you are certain about, then
- In a multiple-choice question, the longest option is usually the right one;
- Unless one of the options is clearly not true, the "all of the above" choice is usually right;

31. In a TRUE/ FALSE question, if the statement is hard to understand it is usually true.

Does the question matter?

The first check of the relevance of an assessment question is to ask a valued employee to sit it. If they do not get it all right, then the questions may be wrong or unnecessary. The second test is to ask a valuable supervisor if this is what employees need to know. The answer will tell you whether you are asking the right questions. The third test is to give the assessment six weeks later to an employee who passed at the training session. This will tell you about recall, but also "do they do it?" and "does it make a difference?"

Do these questions really tell you whether a student learned anything?

32. What does SHMS stand for?

Instead of asking the question this way, ask:

33. What basic elements make up the Safety and Health Management System?

For Queensland coal mines, the answer is in section 6 of the Coal Mining Safety and Health Regulation, 2017. For other industries, there will be relevant workplace health and safety legislation in your jurisdiction, although the terminology, and the answer, may be different.

34. What legislation must a worker in Queensland comply with?

In general, the answer is the "Work Health and Safety Act 2011." If they said "Work Safety and Health Act," would they be wrong? What if they said, "Work Health and Safety Regulation 2011?" That is also a piece of Queensland legislation that deals with workplace safety.

Those laws do not apply to people who work in mines or on petroleum gas leases. Would they be wrong if they said the Coal Mines Safety and Health Regulation? Would they be wrong if they said the Coal Mining Safety and Health Regulation, 2001? How about the Coal Mining Act? A lawyer would be. At the time of writing the answer was the Coal Mining Safety and Health Regulation, 2017. A lawyer's assessments need a different level of precision on that point to the workforce in the industry. The rules that most workers must follow are the procedures written by management and supervisors. These procedures must comply with the legislation, but most of the workforce would not need to see a copy of the regulation very often.

35. Asking questions at the completion of your discussion helps ensure the listeners have understood your information. TRUE / FALSE

Most people would guess TRUE to that, whether they have been trained or not.

Can a candidate at this level understand the question?

36. When communicating you should use language that is:

a) *Clear, succinct and unambiguous*
b) *Undefined and confusing*
c) *Abrupt, hasty and rude*
d) *Clear, succinct and vague*

This question was about clear communication, yet many entry level students, proficient operators or even supervisors may not understand the words succinct, unambiguous or undefined.

37. The planning process includes planning, identification of hazards, hazard risk assessment and control of hazards and risks. This includes the development of procedures for hazard identification, risk assessment and control. TRUE / FALSE

This question had a reading standard of 13.8 years of school and was rated at 22.4% for reading ease. 100% is simple, 0% is extremely hard. I discuss reading ease later in this chapter.

38. Effective communication is crucial particularly in the working environment to avoid misunderstandings. These misunderstandings could at the very least affect efficiency and may have the potential to cause an incident or accident to occur. TRUE / FALSE

This question is also so complex that most people will not bother to read it. But it sounds TRUE.

A valid assessment covers the broad range of knowledge and skills necessary to competently perform the relevant duties?

Is the result reliable?

If another assessor conducted the process with the same candidate would the result be the same? If the same assessor conducted the assessment in another location or on another day, would the result be the same?

A reliable assessment is one where the results are comparable, regardless of who conducts the assessment and where or when it is conducted.

Does it match the level?

The assessment level must match the competency being assessed. In the Australian Quality Training Framework (AQTF), competency level is shown as the first digit in the competency number. For example, RIIRIS402D is a level 4 program. RIIRIS201D is level 2. The level is the first of the three digits after the six letters in the competency name.

The AQTF sets the standard for 7 competency levels in the Vocational Education and Training sector, up to an associate degree. It recognises that the university sector issues qualifications at another 6 levels. In this book I will focus on assessment tasks for levels 2 to 5, although the principles have a wider application.

Certificate 1 qualifications are usually at the pre-employment level. They prepare students for further learning and perhaps internship.

Certificate 2 qualifications are at the entry level to an industry.

People are expected to do routine jobs and follow instructions. They will watch conditions. If things change they will stop work or report the change to a more qualified person. They may follow a different procedure if an expected change occurs.

For mining jobs, a certificate 2 qualified person may work near machinery. They would not usually operate the machine. They may start and stop a conveyor belt. They may read monitoring equipment to help them decide if a place is safe. They may work alone underground in a place that has been inspected. They would need to know how to tell whether the place they were working in was safe. They will also know how to call for help if they need it.

For risk management, the tools that a certificate 2 candidate would be expected to do a personal risk assessment of the hazards that may face or create. They may refer to a group risk assessment that has been prepared with or by others. They might use a risk matrix. They should remember golden rules, or other standards, like "never work under a supported load; always check that power has been isolated; wear protective equipment when working above 1.5 metres off the ground; They would recognise different tags to indicate machine defects and warning tapes to mark exclusion zones.

For communication, they would be able to check with a co-worker or a supervisor. They could use information given at the morning meeting or by the supervisor when they were given the job. They would identify and follow workplace signs, select an item by name or choose the correct tool for a task.

For emergency response, they may have to report what has happened. They can use available equipment such as fire extinguishers or emergency stops to control the emergency. They are familiar with escape routes, and the importance of keeping escape routes clear. They would be able to escape from an unsafe place. They should know the warning levels that affect them and what they should do if the level is reached. They would not be expected to restart equipment until the situation has been checked by a more qualified person.

A question at certificate 2 could ask for a choice between two or more options. A written answer may need five or less words. They could be asked to perform a task that they do on the job. They may be asked to follow a procedure when they perform the task. They could be asked to inspect equipment that they would use on the job.

They would not be expected to carry out a task that does not have a clear procedure. They would be expected to know where to get procedures for tasks that they do.

Certificate 3 qualifications are for people who can do routine jobs under normal conditions. This may include making changes to the way that a job is done if the conditions change. They may operate machinery and carry out routine maintenance tasks by following procedures. They would follow a procedure to check that the machine was able to be used. They monitor the ongoing condition of the workplace and the machinery.

A certificate 3 person would be able to interpret atmospheric or machinery monitoring results and may follow procedures to improve conditions. They may follow fault finding procedures to find the cause of a problem.

If conditions change, they may stop the job they are doing and do work that improve the conditions or stop them getting worse. They report any change in conditions to people working with them and to supervisors.

They may supervise or have responsibility for the work done by other certificate 2 or 3 people.

Certificate 4 qualifications are for people who solve more complex problems. This includes solving an unexpected problem that is not covered in standard procedures and manuals. They will often have a supervisor role and make short term plans.

They inspect the workplace to make sure it is safe for other people to be there. They may change things to make it safe. They may have responsibilities that only they can do. Other supervisors also have responsibilities to make sure that people are working in a safe place and that work is done in a safe way.

Certificate 2, 3 and 4 positions in mining jobs usually work "on the job" for most of the day. Higher certificate qualifications may visit the workplace to check and inspect, give expert advice to the workers and supervisors and make longer term plans.

The qualification certificates go up to level 7, but most of this book is targeted at certificates 2, 3 and 4.

Ethics

An assessor also has ethical responsibilities. They will be given information and observe behaviour and must deal with how they handle these.

Some requirements are set out in legislation, others may come from the organisation's standards and values.

Legislation

Health and safety

The requirement to do an assessment may stress a candidate. In some cases, the assessment may even be designed to simulate the stress that exists in the workplace. As with other factors, it is an ideal that the stress not exceed that which would be encountered on the job. But can you predict or even measure this?

There are other health and safety requirements that must be met. These will vary with the location and the industry, but an assessor should be aware of the legal requirements to report any accidents or "close calls." There may be limits on weights that can be lifted or the quality of air that people may work in, particularly if they are in a confined space. When assessing driving skills, the rules of the road may limit some activities.

Privacy

The Australian Privacy Principles apply to almost all Australian and state government organisations and private companies with an annual turnover of $3 million per year. Some organisations with lower turnover must also comply, for example if they provide health services, deal with personal information or have a government supply contract. As with all legislation, it is regularly updated, so check your privacy obligations regularly. Also, this is a very brief summary of a complex subject. Just because something is not mentioned here it does not mean it is not covered in the law. If something is mentioned, there will probably be other aspects that must be considered. The purpose of this section is only to raise awareness, not to provide advice.

One of the requirements of the legislation is that these organisations must have a privacy policy. The policy must set out how these principles will be applied:

1. Personal information must be handled in an open and transparent way;

2. Where practical, people must have an option to deal with an organisation anonymously or using a pseudonym.
3. Personal information must only be collected where it is necessary for the business to function.
4. If personal information is obtained that is not necessary for the business to function, then it must not be stored.
5. If personal information is obtained, then the person must be notified that business has obtained it.
6. Personal information should only be used for the reason that it was collected.
7. There are restrictions on the use of personal information that has been obtained for business reasons also being used for direct marketing.
8. There are limits on transferring personal information between countries.
9. There are restrictions on the use of government provided numbers as identifiers. This covers passport numbers, drivers licence numbers and Centrelink or Medicare numbers.
10. Steps must be taken to make sure that personal information that is held is accurate and is be kept up to date.
11. Personal information must be stored securely.
12. A person can see personal information that an organisation holds about them and allowed to correct it if it is wrong.

These are just short summaries of complex requirements that an ethical assessor must be aware of.

Check the privacy policy of your organisation to see how it deals with these and other requirements.

Discrimination

There are also strict laws about not treating people differently because of race, colour, gender, sexual orientation, age, physical or mental disability, marital status, family or carer's responsibilities, pregnancy, religion, political opinion, national extraction or social origin.

It is not discrimination if the action is taken because of the nature of the job.

39. Chris is 140 cm tall. A flight attendant helps passengers put bags in overhead lockers. Anyone less than 160 cm tall would not be able to reach the overhead lockers.

- a) Sam is being discriminated against
- b) Height is a job requirement

40. Sally is due to have a baby in three months. Sam is being transferred interstate in 4 months. Sally is not being considered for Sam's position.

- a) Sally is being discriminated against
- b) Being available is a job requirement.

41. Taul is a Bokonist lay preacher. He has been the subject of several complaints about his behaviour at work. While being assessed for a maintenance skill, he dropped and damaged an expensive meter. He was assessed as not yet competent.

- a) Taul is being discriminated against
- b) Taul's assessment was not due to discrimination
- c) There is not enough information to decide.

Organisation and industry standards

Benchmarks are often set by the organisation's policy and by industry standards.

In Queensland mining, there is a recognised standard that deals with training and assessment. Search for "Recognised Standard 11, training in coal mines." Ignore the many suppliers offering to make the qualifications available and choose the option with a web site ending .qld.gov.au. The name of the department changes regularly, but that should give you a good start.

If the range of suppliers distracted you, you may find options to complete the course in between 1 and 5 days. You may even be offered a chance to get your skills on line. Ignore those distractions and have a look at the benchmark standard at the www.qld.gov.au site, by entering Recognised Standard 11 in their search box.

The standard regulates:

- The experience and qualifications of trainers and assessors
- Training needs and pathways
- Recognition of current competencies and prior learning
- Refresher training

For those who are not interested in mining, there is an alternate "Qualifications for correctional services," available on line. You might like to search for it.

Check your own industry requirements. The minimum standards that should be acceptable are:

Trainer and assessor qualifications. They hold a higher competency than the one they are presenting or assessing. There should be an answer to the questions "can the same person train and assess?" This may be industry and subject specific, but if the answer is yes, then what controls are required?

Training needs is a two pronged fork. What does the job require to allow the task to be done competently, productively and safely? What does the candidate require to meet the job requirements?

Current competency means that they are competent to the job elsewhere but need to be assessed in the context of this site. There are two issues that need to be examined: "what are they bringing to this operation? What is happening at this operation that could affect the way they do the task?

Prior Learning is different to current competency. This allows for a range of learning experiences. It may be experience, skill or knowledge.

"How does this fit the current situation?" It must be recognised, but "unlearning" may be as important as learning. What knowledge do they have that has already been identified as inappropriate here, because of improvements, incidents or experience?

Refresher training is required by law in Queensland coal mining. The regulation says,

> … each coal mine worker at a mine, including each worker holding a senior management or supervisory position and each worker holding a certificate of competency, [must be] given refresher training under the mine's training scheme at least once every 5 years.

> The worker must undergo the training.

42. List the reasons why refresher training is necessary

a) *Things have changed*
b) *There are important things I have not done, because I have been busy doing other stuff*
c) *I may have developed habits that are not consistent with good practice*
d) *All of the above*

43. Who should lead refresher training?

a) *Full time trainers*
b) *People who have current experience on the job*

THE CONTEXT

An assessment must relate to the situations that will exist when the task is done "on the job."

Virtual reality may be able to create a realistic environment. I have seen some amazing installations in the Sydney suburban railway training centre and the NSW Coal Services mining training centre. Regrettably, I have also seen some worthless attempts to simulate at the lowest possible cost

I have been told that to fly a modern aircraft requires one pilot and a dog. The pilot is there to feed the dog. The dog's job is to bite the pilot if any controls are touched by a human hand.

It is impossible to predict where technology will take us tomorrow, but I would prefer to be given customer service by a person who was assessed on performance with real customers.

National Competency Standards

The AQTF competencies have been compiled by people who do the job in consultation with other people who do the job. I respect their competence. They have set the following standards in some of competency elements that I reviewed at random:

CPC32413 - Certificate III in Plumbing

> The plumbing industry strongly affirms that training and assessment leading to recognition of skills must be undertaken in a real or very closely simulated workplace

environment and this qualification requires all units of competency to be delivered in this context.

TLIE2007 Use communications systems

Assessment must occur in workplace operational situations where it is appropriate to do so; where this is not appropriate, assessment must occur in simulated workplace operational situations that replicate workplace conditions.

CPPSEC2017A Protect self and others using basic defensive techniques

a setting in the workplace or environment that simulates the conditions of performance described in the elements, performance criteria and range statement.

TLIA1001 Secure cargo

Assessment must occur in workplace operational situations where it is appropriate to do so; where this is not appropriate, assessment must occur in simulated workplace operational situations that replicate workplace conditions.

Here are some examples of how commonly used competency elements can be assessed in context.

Interpret

TAEASS402

1.1. Interpret assessment planning documentation and applicable organisational, legal and ethical requirements for conducting the assessment and confirm with the relevant people

Interpret or apply may mean that you provide a piece of law or a policy or procedure and ask what it means. This question would suit an open book examination.

44. If you were in the situation described in the first column, write "what you would have done about it" in column 2 and give the reference for the paragraph which allows or requires you to do it in column 3.

If	What would you do?	Reference
You have been given a written job instruction that says you must do a job in a particular way. You have often done this job at other places. You know a quick way that is just as safe.		
You work in a place where smoking is not allowed on site. You see a work mate go behind the shed about every two hours. You know he is a smoker.		
There are no pages left in the report book. You have been told to write a report at the end of your job. You were told to take the top copy of the report to the main report room and leave a copy in the lunchroom near the job. There are sheets of blank paper available. You can make up a form that will say the same things as the proper report.		
You caught a bad case of the flu from a friend when you went fishing last week. You have a bad headache, a cough and a runny nose. You will be working close to some other people in a small room.		

Access

ICPDMT263

2.7 Newsgroups relevant to industry are accessed

To test access, you may also need to have an open book exam. What you are testing in this question is whether they can find the answer in the sample text. You are not asking them to do this from memory.

There are a lot of different documents you could use to assess if a candidate can access information. You could use an operators' manual, a maintenance guide, a procedure, a chart or a plan. Here is an example using section 39 of the Coal Mining Safety and Health Act. We also used this section in an earlier question. The section of the act was referred to earlier, in question 21.

45. Which parts of Section 39:

 a) *Apply to visitors to the mine?*
 b) *Mean you cannot work if you are affected by medicine that has been given to you by a doctor?*
 c) *Mean that you must do a SLAM before you start a new job?*
 d) *Say that you must not exceed speed limits on the mine roads?*
 e) *Mean that you must tell your workmate if you think something is unsafe?*

Carry Out

RIICOM201D – Communicate in the workplace

> 1.1 Access, interpret and apply communication site documentation and ensure the work activity is compliant

46. How would you assess the following competency elements for RIICOM201D?

 a) *1 Plan and prepare for workplace communication using equipment and system*
 b) *1.3 Establish and maintain communication with others*
 c) *2 Communicate using communication equipment and systems*
 d) *2.3 Acknowledge and respond to communication*
 e) *2.4 Take, confirm and pass messages on promptly to the others*

f) *2.5 Pass communications in a clear and concise manner*
g) *2.6 Follow safety procedures, including the passing of reports and observance of local communications and emergency procedures*
h) *3 Carry out face-to-face routine communication*
i) *3.5 Participate in discussion to obtain information and clarify meaning*
j) *3.6 Communicate cooperatively and effectively with others*
k) *3.5 Participate in discussion to obtain information and clarify meaning*
l) *3.6 Communicate cooperatively and effectively with others*
m) *4 Complete written documentation*
n) *4.3 Pass on written information to others*

These questions ask mine workers with some experience about how they would carry out the requirements of section 39 of the Coal Mining Safety and Health Act, 1999, without mentioning the act or obligations.

In the next questions I demonstrate how understanding can be confirmed by putting half of the information in the introduction to a multiple choice question and the rest in the option. It is not important that you understand the content, but you should be able to observe the structure of the question and apply it to your subject area.

47. You find out that a roof bolt drill jumps about 2 centimetres while you are drilling a hole for secondary support. Who do you need to tell? Mark all the people you must tell. Some of those people will tell others in the list. Only mark the ones you must tell.

a) *Other mine workers who are working nearby*
b) *Your supervisor*
c) *The Deputy for the district*
d) *The Site Safety and Health Representative.*
e) *Control*
f) *The Geotechnical Engineer*
g) *The Site Senior Executive*
h) *The Underground Mine Manager*

OR

48. You have found a hot roller on a conveyor belt. What information would you need to get so that you could report it report to control?

OR

49. You have been told not to go through the trapdoor near where you are working, because the longwall is working. Another mineworker is heading towards the trapdoor, what would you do?

For this you question may leave it as a short answer question (level 3 or above) or you may give choices (for levels 2 and 3):

- a) *Tell the other person that you have been told not to go through that door*
- b) *Tell the other person not to go through the trapdoor, because the longwall is working*
- c) *Say nothing, just keep doing your job*
- d) *Report to control that the person has gone through the trapdoor*
- e) *Tell your supervisor the person went through the door, the next time you see them.*

These next questions are suitable for an inexperienced worker, who has had the obligations under section 39 explained. (see question 21)

50. You are in the lunchroom. There are two other people there that you do not know. The phone is ringing. Neither of them has answered it. You are the closest person to the phone. What would you do?

This question builds on their experience away from mining. They will have heard a phone ring unanswered. The polite thing to do is different to what is expected at an underground mine.

OR

51. List 3 ways that you might be given information about the safety of the place where you are going to work.

They should be able to visualise a pre-shift meeting, a supervisor that can be asked questions, or notice boards setting out safety information.

OR

52. List 3 things you must do if you are concerned about the safety of the place where you have been asked to work.

Again, the idea of isolation tape, tagging or a written report, verbal report to a supervisor and phoning control should be within their experience.

DESIGN

Throughout this book I have provided examples of many different designs for assessment activities. What I cannot provide is the content for your instruments. Opportunities for quality design may be identified by supervisors, practitioners, subject matter experts and from the candidates. Never underrate the potential contribution of a future candidate in the design process. They can offer examples of both best practice and poor practice. They may be able to suggest short cuts which present opportunities or inspire prohibitions.

You may gather content from

- Organisational policies
- Procedures for activities
- Operator manuals
- Promotional material
- News articles
- Internet sites
- Legal and ethical requirements
- Community expectations
- Objectives of the organisation at a macro level, and the action that is being taken at the local level.
- The ability of the candidate that is being assessed

Assessment instruments should be reviewed by people who competently perform the task and supervisors or customers who receive the output.

Each instrument should include instructions to the assessor, particularly if there are time limits or pass marks.

Content

53. Which of these must be included in your candidate briefing?

a) Time limits
b) How the answer is to be provided
c) Available tools or assistance
d) Restrictions on using tools or assistance
e) How they will be given feedback
f) What information other people will be given about their performance.

As part of the design process, ask a valued employee who uses the skill and a valuable supervisor who appreciates the results of the activity to do the assessment. Ask whether the questions are valid, sufficient, authentic and current.

EVIDENCE

This book provides examples of many ways that evidence can be collected.

A large proportion of our examples assess knowledge. This may be done by written instrument, face to face interview, inspection of items that have been produced, review of tasks that have been undertaken, reading reports or in many other ways. No matter how the assessment is developed, the evidence must be

- Sufficient
- Authentic, and
- Current.

Sufficient

Are you gathering enough information to accurately assess the candidate?

The oral examination panel that assesses competency for Queensland mine managers covers different subjects and lasts at least three hours. We develop a major mining scenario and then assess the candidate's response in each of the competency areas, which includes ventilation, gas control, roof support, emergency response and legal compliance.

It is possible to dramatically adjust the answer to the question by making minor changes to the mine plan, so we could use the same basic scenario for several candidates. On one occasion we had a brand new scenario and a candidate that none of us on the panel had previously examined. The candidate answered all of our questions in an hour and a half. Had we set a question that was too easy? We added some extra questions and kept the candidate busy for another 30 minutes.

When we reviewed the performance we all agreed that this was an exceptional candidate. It was confirmed by the next one, who when given a slightly adjusted question was unable to provide a solution in close to four hours.

So, the measure of sufficiency will often be more than just time spent.

In the competency elements for the AQTF Workplace Assessor skill set, several assessment activities are prescribed:

> For **TAEASS402 Contribute to assessment,** "carrying out a minimum of three evidence-gathering activities and, on each occasion, document evidence in a clear and concise manner and document feedback from others involved in the assessment."
>
> For **TAEASS402 Plan assessment activities and processes,** "The candidate must demonstrate the ability to complete tasks outlined in the elements and performance criteria of this unit, including planning and organising the assessment process on a minimum of five separate occasions and planning and organising two Recognition of Prior Learning (RPL) assessments (which may be two of the five assessment processes above.)"
>
> For **TAEASS402 Assess competence,** there are several measured requirements:
>
> - assessment of at least five candidates within the vocational education and training (VET) context against at least one endorsed or accredited unit of competency according to the organisation's assessment processes and practices.
> - using recognition of prior learning (RPL) processes in the assessment of at least one candidate (which may be one of the five candidates above)
> - making reasonable adjustments in the assessment of at least one candidate

Authentic

Do your questions measure what you intend to measure?

If your assessments are competency based, are you testing the ability to do the job or are you testing knowledge, which may be perfectly accurate, but is not relevant to the task that is being performed?

To show the difference between education and competence, consider which of these occupations would require the knowledge listed in question 54 to perform their job competently:

1. A workplace safety inspector
2. A motor mechanic
3. A medical doctor
4. A forensic pathologist
5. A workshop supervisor
6. A chemist in a laboratory where explosives are tested
7. A fire fighter
8. An air conditioning installer

54. Match the following facts with the needs of each of the occupations listed above.

a) *The chemical formula for Carbon Monoxide is CO*
b) *The maximum allowable concentration of Carbon Monoxide in a workplace is 30 parts per million, where the worker is exposed for five, consecutive, eight-hour shifts.*
c) *Carbon monoxide is a deadly gas that is present in motor vehicle exhausts.*
d) *The most common symptoms of CO poisoning are headache, dizziness, weakness, upset stomach, vomiting, chest pain, and confusion.*
e) *The symptoms of CO poisoning are often described as "flu-like."*
f) *If you breathe in a lot of CO it can make you pass out or kill you.*
g) *People who are sleeping or drunk can die from CO poisoning before they have symptoms.*

h) *Infants, the elderly, people with chronic heart disease, anaemia, or breathing problems are more likely to get sick from CO*
i) *A small leak in a car exhaust system can lead to a build up of CO inside the car.*
j) *Ventilation systems are an effective way to remove carbon monoxide from the workplace.*
k) *Protective respiratory equipment is available for many gases, including Carbon Monoxide.*
l) *The Relative Density of Carbon Monoxide is 0.97. The Relative Density of air is 1.*
m) *Carbon Monoxide is explosive in the range 12.5% to 75%.*
n) *Regardless of the level of exposure, practically all carbon monoxide is eliminated from the bloodstream within eight to ten hours after exposure ends.*
o) *The removal of carbon monoxide from the haemoglobin is accelerated by the inhalation of oxygen.*
p) *A victim of CO poisoning should be kept lying down and warm in an area away from draft.*
q) *After any exposure to carbon monoxide poisoning, the victim should be treated by a physician and may need to go to hospital.*
r) *The Encyclopaedia of Occupational Safety and Health. 3rd ed, published by the International Labor Office, Geneva, in 1983. lists CO poisoning as the most single cause of poisoning in both industry and the home.*
s) *Accurate field and laboratory techniques exist for both blood and expired air measurement which show good correlation with each other*
t) *The concentration of Carbon Monoxide in a room where cigarettes are being smoked may reach 15 parts per million*
u) *The concentration of Carbon Monoxide on a busy city intersection may reach 50 parts per million*
v) *At a concentration of 10 to 20 % Carboxyhaemoglobin, a casualty may suffer from tightness across the forehead or a slight headache.*
w) *At a concentration of 60 to 70 % Carboxyhaemoglobin, a casualty may suffer from Coma with intermittent convulsions, depressed respiration and heart action and possibly death.*
x) *A person who smokes one packet of cigarettes a day will have a level of 5 to 6 per cent Carboxyhaemoglobin in their bloodstream.*

y) *The content for this series of questions came from the Worksafe Australia Hazardous Chemical Information page for Carbon Monoxide. An up to date copy can be obtained by searching for this page on the internet.*

Current

The questions or activities in an assessment can become dated as new information becomes available. The 2005 Nobel Prize in Medicine was won by Barry J. Marshall and J. Robin Warren for their discovery of "the bacterium Helicobacter pylori and its role in gastritis and peptic ulcer disease."

Before their discovery, stress and lifestyle were considered the causes of the condition. The disease was treated by reducing gastric acid production. The treatment worked but did not prevent reinfection. The award winners found that the condition was infectious.

Perhaps not every change in the content you are assessing will result in a Nobel Prize. As organisations make continual improvements in processes, introduce new products and services or remove items from the range, the assessment material must be updated.

Continuing professional development and maintenance of competency rely on refresher training. This should be targeted at things people are likely to have forgotten because they have not used the knowledge or skill and things that have changed. Lack of use of knowledge is not a reason for removing it from the curriculum. Often highest impact events are the least frequent. We don't remove the fire exits, just because there has not been a fire in the building. We do hold periodic fire drills to remind people of the process.

MAPPING THE ASSESSMENT TO A COMPETENCY

A single question may test knowledge on several items of competency.

Here is a partial map of a competency assessment.

As you can see in the 6 questions referred to in the sample there is confirmation of many of the competency elements. 4 Questions would give confirmed evidence of 6 elements.

RIIERR302D - Respond to local emergencies and incidents		1	2	3	4	5	6
1. Plan and prepare to respond to local emergencies and incidents	1.1 Access, interpret and apply local emergencies and incidents documentation and ensure the work activity is compliant	X	X	X			
	1.2 Obtain, read, interpret, clarify and confirm work requirements				X	X	
	1.3 Identify and address potential risks, hazards and environmental issues and implement control measures				X	X		X
	1.4 Select and wear personal protective equipment appropriate for work activities						X	
	1.5 Identify, establish and maintain communication systems with other personnel during the emergency	X	X	X			X

		1	2	3	4	5	6
	1.6 Communicate and coordinate activities with others prior to, during and on completion of the work activity				X		X
	1.7 Locate, obtain and test emergency equipment					X	

The same 6 questions also deal with a large proportion of the knowledge and skills requirements for the unit.

In the next section, I have also mapped the questions against Bloom's Taxonomy, using the code:

A: Awareness
K: Knowledge
U: Understanding
S: Skills, to avoid confusing application with awareness.

Performance Evidence

		1	2	3	4	5	6
Evidence is required to be collected that demonstrates a candidate's competency in this unit. Evidence must be relevant to the roles within this sector's work operations and satisfy all of the requirements of the performance criteria of this unit and include that the candidate:	locates and applies relevant documentation, policies and procedures	A		S			
implements the requirements, procedures and techniques for the safe, effective and efficient completion of responding to local emergencies and incidents including:	identifying hazards		U			S	

Outcome	Sub-criterion						
	identifying, analysing and reporting emergencies/incidents	A	K	A			
	monitoring and assessing emergency situations			S			K
	assessing situation and making decisions			S			
	assessing and managing risks						
works effectively with others to undertake and complete the response to local emergencies and incidents that meets all the required outcomes including:	complying with written and verbal reporting requirements and procedures			K			
	communicating clearly and concisely with others to receive and clarify work instructions	S	U	S			
	communicating clearly and concisely with others to coordinate work activities			S			
demonstrates completion of the response to local emergencies and incidents that safely, effectively and efficiently meets all of the required outcomes on more than one (1) occasion including:	reading and interpreting site plans						

	administering initial response First Aid					
	locating and wearing personal protective equipment				K	
	following emergency evacuation procedures	A	A	A		
	applying fire fighting techniques				K	
	isolating sources of danger and placing signage/barriers/ signals as necessary					
	selecting and using emergency equipment	U	U		U	S

This is only part of the assessment map, which covered 18 elements through 14 questions.

For the benefit of trainers, when you write the answer guide, show the source of the answer. Then the trainer can prepare background information or explain the context of the information that is being given. One way that I do this is add a list of regulation clauses or safety alerts to the assessment map.

From an assessment perspective there may be no need to ask a question for each competency element. Firstly, one question can address several elements, and secondly assessment is only a sampling technique. The volume of data gathered may not increase the amount of valid information obtained. When developing training or assessments, I try to remember that not all data is information; not all information is knowledge and not all knowledge is wisdom.

A by product of trying to match each competency element with a question results in meaningless questions like these:

1.3 Identify and address potential risks, hazards and environmental issues and implement control measures

55. In an emergency or incident situation, important issues are the delegation of duties, minimising casualties, effective rescue and treatment, minimising damage to the property and the environment.
True / False

1.5 Identify, establish and maintain communication systems with other personnel during the emergency

56. Explain effective communication and why it is so essential in an emergency situation.

1.6 Communicate and coordinate activities with others prior to, during and on completion of the work activity

**57. You must follow site policies and procedures for communications.
True / False**

The questions, taken from an actual assessment, range from the simplest of guessable TRUE/FALSE questions to a request for a dissertation to a question even less meaningful than the "effective communication" asked for.

SAMPLES

Paired choice

A True / False question is a choice between two options. It should never be just a slab of text from the legislation or text book.

Even a person familiar with the legislation may have difficulty telling whether this statement is true or false:

58. Is this statement TRUE or FALSE?

> *A high potential incident is an event that has the potential to cause an accident.*

A candidate may know that section 17 of the act says:

> A high potential incident at a coal mine is an event, or a series of events, that causes or has the potential to cause a significant adverse effect on the safety or health of a person.

And that section 15 of the same act says

> An accident at a coal mine is an event, or a series of events, at the coal mine causing injury to a person.

All the information is contained in the TRUE / FALSE statement, but a person who is knowledgeable about the legislation may argue it is false, because "an accident," as defined, is not necessarily "a significant adverse effect on the safety or health of a person." You can avoid this by moving away from TRUE / FALSE statements and instead using other terms.

For example,

59. Do you have to stop work immediately and report to your supervisor if there has been an event that could easily have caused an accident if someone had been in a different place? YES / NO

You may give a set of choices

    a   Yes, always
    b   Only is someone is hurt
    c   If any equipment is damaged

60. You have seen an event which could very easily have been an accident. You are concerned that it could happen again. Would you:

    a) Report it to your supervisor the next time you see them?
    b) Report it to the control room the next time you are near a phone
    c) Stop work immediately and report it to your supervisor.
    d) Do what you need to get things back to normal and keep working

These questions assess the action that must be taken when you see a High Potential Incident. This is more likely the reason for the training, rather than just knowing the definition.

Another way of putting TRUE / FALSE questions may be to pack several together in a Matched Choice question.

Matched Choice

This type of question can be used to see if candidates understand their responsibilities or obligations.

61. Match the person who must make the inspection with what is inspected. There may be more than one person for each question.

A deputy is a mine official who makes inspections and evaluates working conditions.

Who must:	Mineworker	Supervisor	Deputies
See if it is safe to continue working after the ventilation has stopped			
See if the fire extinguisher on the machine the mineworker is driving is charged			
Check the methane level when driving a vehicle in a return airway			
Check the water pressure on a conveyor belt firefighting line			
Measure the distance between roof bolts when placing secondary support.			
See if the ribs are safe before placing extra rib bolts.			
Inspect the section of the mine before people start work there. This may be done on an earlier shift.			
Inspect the place where you are working while you are working there.			
Check for gas where you are working while you are working there.			

62. Are these conditions Hazards or Controls?

This type of question may check understanding of the definition of two associated but different terms. Some conditions may be both.

Write YES here if this could be a HAZARD	Condition	Write YES here if this could be a CONTROL
	The plate on a rib bolt can be moved by hand	
	A siren is sounding	
	There is a NO ENTRY sign on the door to the gas monitoring room.	
	The support rules say that roof bolts are placed 1 metre apart. There is a section of the roof where it is almost two metres between bolts.	
	The seal is missing on the first aid equipment. It was there yesterday.	
	There is CAUTION tape across a roadway.	
	There is a radio blackspot in part of the mine where you will be working.	

Multiple Choice

This type of question asks for a choice between several options. It is suitable for assessments of level 2 candidates and above.

Common problems with multiple choice questions are that:

- The longest option is the correct one;

- Where "all of the above" is an option, it is usually the correct one. It is often difficult to set an option that is not clearly incorrect. "all of the above" is often used because it is too hard to produce other suitable options.
- Ridiculous options are included to pad out the numbers. See Question 44.

Instead of using "all of the above," say "more than one option may be marked."

Sometimes multiple choice questions are necessary so that the answers can be given with small handheld keypads or entered at a kiosk by people with limited typing skill. The answers are recorded in the computer system. This technology allows higher quality choices using video clips and photos. It should not make it necessary to introduce ridiculous questions.

Here are some examples using a picture or a photo. On a computer screen, the options can be provided in colour at no extra cost.

| Danger tag | Out of service Tag | Information tag |
| (Red & white) | (Yellow and Black) | (Blue & white) |

63. Which tag would you use?

a) *The battery powered drill you need to do your job has been checked by the engineers and they said it is OK to take underground. What sort of tag would they put on?*

b) *The transport vehicle is needed for the manager to take visitors underground in about two hours' time. You have been told to put a tag on it so that people know it is not to be used.*
c) *The brakes on the machine you have been using are not working. You told your supervisor it is dangerous. He said to put a tag on it.*
d) *You will be working near a conveyor belt. You are worried that people may not notice you are there and start the belt.*

If you use tapes or signs to restrict access, ask the trainee to select from the sign or tape in your list. Again, pictures will help.

| Caution Tape (Yellow & black) | Danger Tape (Red & white) | Restricted tape (Blue & White) |

64. Which tape means?

a) *Take extra care when working here*
b) *Do not enter this area*
c) *Do not enter this place unless the supervisor says you can*
d) *No vehicles may go past this place*
e) *Do not pass here unless you have signed the access permit*

65. Which tape would you use if?

a) *You will be working on the roadway and you do not want vehicles to come past*
b) *There is deep water across the roadway near this place*
c) *You will be working above this place and may drop your tools*
d) *You will be working on a step on the other side of a door. The door must stay closed. Many people have keys to the door.*

66. Who can put up this sort of tape?

   a) *Any worker*
   b) *A supervisor*
   c) *A worker who has been trained*
   d) *The worker who found the danger*

67. Who can remove this type of barrier tape?

   a) *Any worker*
   b) *A supervisor*
   c) *A worker who has been trained*
   d) *The worker who found the danger*

Here is an example of ridiculous options I found in an induction assessment.

68. List the personal protective equipment you must wear when you are in the workshop

   a) *Jacket, hat, long sleeve shirt*
   b) *Safety glasses, closed-in footwear, hi-vis clothing, gloves*
   c) *Footy shorts, singlet, cap*
   d) *All of the above.*

For a question like this it would be better to ask the candidate to list the items. Where literacy may be an issue is not an option, photos of people, with only one correctly dressed would be a suitable way to check understanding. Incorrect picture answers may show some wearing loose fitting clothing, jewellery or carrying prohibited items.

Prepare work plans

Level 2 and 3 competencies may require you to prepare a plan, by following procedures.

You may ask questions about

- where to find procedures;
- the procedure for developing and changing a procedure.
- requirements for inspections to be done
- reports that must be made

A combination of these can be built into a question.

69. A class of schoolchildren will be visiting the workplace next Thursday. You have been asked to make arrangements.

   a) *What procedures apply when children are on site?*
   b) *How will the need for protective equipment apply?*
   c) *What areas need to be isolated?*
   d) *What permits are required?*
   e) *What reports must be completed?*

This is not a multiple choice question, but a series of short answer questions about activities that have to be done.

Induction programs

Many level 2 programs are for people who have not worked in the industry yet. Every business and industry has its jargon and acronyms. Question 1 highlighted the difference in the meaning of words used in mining.

An induction program, sometimes called onboarding or orientation aims to integrate the new people into the team as quickly as possible. Avoid, at all costs, the tendency to unleash an information dump. I saw one program where new starters were given 115 pages of forms and questions to be completed over two days. There were over 300 questions, mostly multiple choice. In addition, there were also 37 practical activities that were to be observed and a further 6 pages of single line items which the assessor was asked to mark for each candidate as Competent or Not Yet Competent.

All this in their first days on the job, when the most important questions to the candidates were "where are the bathrooms and what time is lunch?"

I hope that the designers do not think that regime offers any sort of protection against accidents. All it does is creates an impression that here is a place where training is a formality and records are the priority.

If you really want to integrate new people, have your senior staff drop by to say hello. Show them how things work. Answer their questions.

If you want to highlight particular processes that you regard as important then start with a comparison with an activity they are familiar with.

In mining, we ask all employees to regularly conduct personal safety awareness checks. To prepare them to do it in an unfamiliar setting, I ask them to do it in a setting that is familiar. I ask a question that relates to experience that most people have. For example, refuelling a car, replacing a light globe, or changing a wheel.

RIIGOV201D:
1.3 Prepare work plans that will ensure compliance with procedures and safe work outcomes

70. What order will you do these tasks in if you are refuelling your car at a service station?

    a) *Apply the handbrake*
    b) *Return the nozzle to the pump*
    c) *Replace the cap*
    d) *Turn off the engine*
    e) *Squeeze the handle*
    f) *Release the squeeze*
    g) *Remove the cap*

RIIRIS201D

2.4 Assess risk against criteria to identify if it calls for 'unacceptable risk' status and action

To assess against this element, I have used some practical examples that would be within most people's experience.

71. You are doing a safety analysis before refuelling your car. Tick (✓) the steps that you believe do not have an acceptable level of risk and must not be done while you are refuelling the car.

   a) Drink a bottle of water
   b) Make a mobile phone call
   c) Smoke cigarette
   d) Light a cigarette
   e) Drink a cup of coffee
   f) Latch the trigger in the on position
   g) Eat an apple

Applying criteria

The criteria used by miners to assess risk are "consequences" and "likelihood."

Consequences deal with what will happen if things go wrong. For miners a scale of 5 ranges from "no injury to a fatality:

1. No injury
2. Injury needing first aid treatment
3. Injury needing medical attention
4. Injury leading to long term disability
5. Fatal injury.

The likelihood ranges from extremely rare to common. We will grade them as A to E:

   A. Very unlikely. Rare

B. Could happen
C. Sometimes happens
D. Often happens
E. Usually happens

This is called a matrix. For this question I have given an example.

72. Use the Risk Matrix to estimate the level of risk:

Example:

   a) *A 12 year old child riding a skateboard down a hill near your house. (you choose the hill)*

The likelihood of bruised knees is high – so the risk could be assessed as 2D

   b) *Smoking a cigarette while refuelling a lawn mower at home*
   c) *Bathing a 3 week old baby*
   d) *Cleaning the leaves from the gutter of a Queenslander style home*
   e) *Swimming at a beach where marine stingers were seen last week.*

Controls are ways that risk can be managed. Again, I have given an example.

73. List 3 controls that you would use to reduce the risk for each these cases:

   a) *Teaching a teenager to drive a car*
   - Early lessons on very quiet roads
   - Only the instructor and the trainee in the car
   - Early lessons in daylight in fine weather
   b) *Fishing from a bridge*
   c) *Driving behind a road train along a winding road*
   d) *Allowing your teenage child to go on a first date*
   e) *Buying a used car*

Question layout

These samples show different ways that questions may be laid out. They do not necessarily match any competency standards, but many have been set against requirements of Queensland coal mining safety and health legislation. See if you can use these samples to form a question that tests the knowledge or skill that you want to assess.

Short Answer Questions

These are most useful where there is a definite answer. If the answer is more than three or four words, there may be problems with interpretation of the answer.

74. After what length of roadway driveage (in metres) must it be treated with an explosion inhibitor?

75. In what period after it is driven (in hours) must a roadway be treated with explosion inhibitor?

By nominating the units as "hours" or "metres" a wrong "correct" answer is avoided. Both hours and metres may be referred to as length.

76. A machine is fitted with two automatic gas detectors, one to detect the concentration near the cutters (Detector A) and another detector to detect the concentration in the general area (Detector B). At what concentration, measured on Detector A, must the electricity supply to the cutters trip?

If there are several details that affect the answer, include some of the details in the question. There is too much detail in this question to include it in the short answer list that deals with gas levels in question 84.

77. List 3 hazards associated with using explosives and the controls that are used to reduce the risk.

Hazard: _____

Control: _____

This question tests both knowledge of the regulation and understanding of risk management terms, hazard and control.

Short Answer Lists

Sometimes a series of different answers on related matter can be assessed from a short answer list:

78. What is the normal speed limit in the following places:

  a) On a main suburban road passing a school, during the hour before school starts and for an hour after school finishes?
  b) On a minor suburban road passing a school during school hours?
  c) On a main intercity highway passing through a small town
  d) In a suburban area in a major city

Questions that match lists

The information for the next questions, comes from "Australian Qualifications Framework," published by the Australian Qualifications Framework Council in January 2013. It can be downloaded from the internet. As names change over time, search for the title and if necessary, the edition.

79. What level graduate would you expect to have

  a) *theoretical and practical knowledge and skills for specialised or skilled work?*

b) *basic factual, technical and procedural knowledge of a defined area of work and learning*
c) *select and apply a specialised range of methods, tools, materials and information to complete routine activities*
d) *demonstrate autonomy and limited judgement in structured and stable contexts*

The content for these questions came from the summary on page 12 of the framework document.

If this table was the subject of a lesson, these questions confirm the student's knowledge of the grade levels, which was not specifically asked for, and their understanding ranges across "knowledge, skills and application."

If the table has been provided as a practical activity to confirm research skills, the amount of time taken to complete the activity could be one test of the candidate's understanding. Someone who was unfamiliar with the concepts may need to read every item, while someone familiar with the material would hone in on the relevant text.

This test would not check interpretation or analysis, as the words are direct quotes from the source.

For a level 2 or 3 candidate, presented with a similar block of information, a timed test may indicate their skill at finding and matching information that they are not familiar with.

Where an assessment is to determine the best choice between options, this type of table is useful. Allocate letters to the options, against a brief description, then ask for those letters to be allocated to the best option. This could be used for matching a customer's wants with a choice from a product, such as a new car or a holiday booking. I used the tail end of the alphabet, in capital letters to name the options, to avoid confusing with the numbers of the sub-questions.

80. Schedule 4 of the Regulation refers to ventilation control devices.

Code	Features
V	Antistatic, fire resistant and of substantial construction providing for minimal leakage
W	Antistatic and fire resistant
X	Capable of withstanding an overpressure of 35 kPa
Y	Capable of withstanding an overpressure of 70 kPa
Z	Capable of withstanding an overpressure of 14 kPa for its useful life

81. Match the type of stopping with its features, using the codes in the table:

 a) *A brattice line or temporary stopping*
 b) *A mine entry airlock, while it is open*
 c) *Ventilation ducting*
 d) *A separation stopping for a primary escapeway*
 e) *A stopping, overcast or regulator installed as part of the main ventilation system*
 f) *A stopping, overcast or regulator installed as part of the ventilation system for a panel*

There are 5 options to answer 6 questions. This avoids choosing the last one standing if you know most of the answers.

The Code V – Z is used to avoid confusion with type B, C, D and E seals, referred to in the legislation and to keep away from the convention for naming sub-questions.

The expression "for its useful life" is used instead of "for the life of the panel" to reduce the size of the hint

The expression "while it is open" is moved from the "Features" to the "Type" to avoid giving a hint.

Tables

Missing cells in a table can be used to determine knowledge of related information. This chart is an example of a series of questions formatted in a table:

82. Before the explosives are first used at the mine, the site senior executive must ensure a risk assessment is carried out to identify—
(a) the hazards involved in transporting, storing and using explosives; and
(b) the ways of effectively controlling the hazards.

83. Use this table to list some of the hazards and controls required under the regulation. Some hazards may be controlled in several ways and some controls may apply to several hazards. Place at least 1 response in each numbered cell and at least 8 responses between the 6 numbered cells

Hazard	Control
The explosives are not suitable for use in coal mines	
Unused explosives are left underground	
	a flashing red light, or other warning device, to mark an underground explosive storage
A discrepancy between the amount of explosives issued from surface magazines and the explosives used or stored underground	
	Protection against impact
Detonation by radio transmission	

84. Complete the cells in this table:

Name of Gas	Chemical formula	Lower explosive limit	Upper explosive limit	Long term exposure limit	Maximum exposure limit
Methane		5%		Not toxic	
	CO_2				
		4%	74%		
Hydrogen Sulphide					
	NO_2				
		12.5%	74%	30 ppm	Not set in regulation
Nitric Oxide					
Nitrous Oxide					Not set in regulation
	SO_2	Not Explosive			
Mineral Oil Mist	Complex mixture	Not Explosive			

This table allows you to set the order of accuracy expected (Lower Explosive Limit for methane 5%, not 4.97) and how to deal with responses that don't match the standard (e.g. "Not set in regulation", "Not explosive"). It also allows you to exclude some cells ("Complex Mixture" is given as the answer for a formula so that people don't try to provide one.)

Multiple Choice Questions

Multiple choice questions are popular because they are easy to mark and easy to answer. Unfortunately, they are difficult to prepare. The questions on the following two pages are all poor examples. An explanation of why they are poor follows each set of questions.

85. Where must the alarm activated by the methane detector on a booster fan be?

   a) *A place that allows the necessary action to be taken promptly*
   b) *On the surface of the mine*
   c) *In the mine control room*
   d) *In a place that is staffed all day every day.*

This is an example of badly worded options.

All those answers could be right. The wording from the regulation is option (a).

Try to make all options about the same length. Often the correct answer is easily guessed because it is the longest one.

86. Where must the alarm activated by the methane detector on a booster fan be?

   a) *A place that allows the necessary action to be taken promptly*
   b) *Where it is easily accessible by a person checking the condition of the fan*
   c) *In a security monitoring station away from the mine that is staffed 24/7*
   d) *On the surface, at the mine site in a control room that is staffed 24/7*

This is another example of badly worded options

Option (b) is the location described in the regulation or other monitoring equipment on a booster fan, so a person familiar with the regulation could easily make the mistake of thinking that this applies to the methane detector too. Under some conditions, it may be correct. But option (a) is the wording in the legislation.

While it may be OK to use text book answers as correct options, you must be careful if you use text book answers to other questions for the wrong options.

Either option (c) or (d) could be correct. The regulation does not specify the location, as long as prompt action can be taken.

Avoid jargon terms like 24/7 unless it is common jargon in the place where the people being assessed work. "Staffed all day every day" is likely to be understood by most people. 24/7 may not be. To miners, it could look like a demanding roster – 24 days on 7 off.

87. When you are near a continuous miner that is cutting coal, NO STANDING ZONE means:

   a) *Only the machine operator may work or stand there*
   b) *Only experienced face workers may work or stand there*
   c) *Only people who have permission from the machine operator may work or stand there*
   d) *No one may work or stand there*

88. When you are near a continuous miner that is cutting coal, CONTROL ZONE means:

   a) *Only the machine operator may work or stand there*
   b) *Only experienced face workers may work or stand there*
   c) *Only people who have permission from the machine operator may work or stand there*
   d) *No one may work or stand there*

89. When a continuous miner is being serviced, NO STANDING ZONE means:

   a) *Only people who have attached personal danger locks to the main isolator may work or stand there*
   b) *Only experienced face workers may work or stand there*
   c) *Only people who have permission from the machine operator may work or stand there*
   d) *No one may work or stand there*

90. Where is the NO STANDING ZONE while the miner is being maintained? The miner has been isolated

Tick all correct answers

   a) From the back of the shovel to the face
   b) From the back of the shovel to 5 metres in front of the picks
   c) On top of the miner
   d) Between the miner and the rib
   e) From 5 metres behind the miner to the back of the shovel
   f) NO STANDING ZONES do not apply if the miner is isolated
   g) NO STANDING ZONES do not apply if the miner is isolated and the person has put a personal lock on the main isolator

91. When a continuous miner is in bolting mode, CONTROL ZONE means:

   a) Only people who have attached personal danger locks to the main isolator may work or stand there
   b) Only experienced face workers may work or stand there
   c) Only people who have permission from the machine operator may work or stand there
   d) No one may work or stand there

Questions 92 to 96 are examples which assess a clear understanding of the difference between two or three terms that are used together.

This is a better option than TRUE / FALSE questions.

Another use for multiple choice questions is to ask the meaning of definitions.

92. Guttering is

   a) Special cuts in the floor to carry water
   b) Broken roof along the side of a roadway
   c) A stone band in the seam which is usually wet

93. Full encapsulation means

   a) *Putting more than one capsule in the hole*
   b) *Plastic or fibreglass bolts are used*
   c) *The bolt is coated with resin for its full length*

94. Cable bolts

   a) *are flexible, longer bolts usually set as secondary support*
   b) *are used for rib support on the block that will be cut by the shearer*
   c) *are placed in the rib to hang cables and hoses on*

In questions 93 and 94 a term in the definition ("capsule" or "cable") is repeated in an incorrect option. This may encourage the untrained person to guess that option. If you use this type of question often, sometimes you should include the repeated word in a correct option, so that people who guess you won't use the same word in the correct answer will be caught out.

Ordered Lists

95. You need to take a vehicle through double ventilation doors that open in the direction you are travelling. There is no powered door opening device available.

Place the number 1 next to the first thing you would do, 2, next to the second and so on in the order you would do them.

Mark anything that you would not do as 0.

   a) __ *Turn off any automatic methane detector on the machine*
   b) __ *Close the first door*
   c) __ *Close the second door*
   d) __ *Open the first door by hand*
   e) __ *Open the second door by hand*

f) ___ Gently push the first door open with the vehicle
g) ___ Gently push the second door open with the vehicle
h) ___ Turn off any automatic methane detectors in the roadway
i) ___ Stop the vehicle before you reach the first door
j) ___ Stop the vehicle before you reach the second door
k) ___ Drive through the first doorway
l) ___ Drive through the second doorway

The letters before the questions are only there for this discussion. They would not appear in the assessment paper.

Option (h) introduces extra knowledge that an operator may not connect. Because the doors open in the direction of travel, you would be going from a return to an intake. An automatic methane detector is required in the returns. It may not be needed in the intake. You would not normally turn it off, though. In fact, you cannot turn them off. A number on option (h) would be enough to mark the whole question wrong.

Pushing doors with a vehicle is bad practice. Again, a number on question (f) or (g) would mean the whole answer is wrong.

96. A flammable gas detector is showing a high alarm. When you try to shut down the diesel vehicle, it will not shut down normally. What will you do?

Number the answers in the order you would do them.

Mark anything that you would not do as 0.

Mark anything that you would only do if everything else failed as X

a) ___ Drive the vehicle to a place where the alarm is off
b) ___ Leave the vehicle where it is and take the detector with you to a place where the alarm is off

c) __ *Fill the fuel tank with water*
d) __ *Cut the fuel lines*
e) __ *Put an Out of Service Tag on the vehicle*
f) __ *Turn the vehicle off at the strangler valve*
g) __ *Drain the scrubber tank so that the engine will cut out*
h) __ *Remove the air filter and jam a rag into the inlet*

Options (c) (d) and (h) are absolute desperation steps. Option (e) is normally the last step. Fix the problem first, then place the tag. In this case option (a) would only be considered when absolutely everything else has failed, so it is a last choice. (g) is not an option. Draining the scrubber tank may remove the flameproof protection so should not be done.

True / False or Paired choice

Many True / False questions have obvious answers. There is a 50% chance that a guess will be right anyway.

97. A competent person is a person who has demonstrated skill and knowledge required to carry out a task to a standard necessary for the safety and health of persons. TRUE / FALSE

This is an example of badly worded question

Is there a person alive who is likely to be assessed on this subject who would answer false to that question? Really?

98. Each training package should have a lesson plan that outlines the process for completing the training and assessment. Appointed trainers and assessors shall follow the lesson plan. TRUE / FALSE

99. A coal mine worker required to undertake a designated task is required to be assessed as competent and authorised in writing by the General Manager. TRUE / FALSE

Questions 97 to 99 came from an assessment for trainers and assessors. None is likely to be answered incorrectly.

Here are some examples of paired choices which do require knowledge.

100. Compressed air may only be used to clean clothing, body and hair if the nozzle outlet is less than 10 mm wide – TRUE / FALSE

This may be credible to someone who has not had any training in the subject, particularly because the 10 mm part makes it sound official.

101. If a person who is mentioned in the management structure for a coal mine is temporarily absent from duty, another competent person to do those duties only needs to be appointed if the absence is for more than 14 days. TRUE / FALSE

This confirms that they understand the difference between the absence of the General Manager and the absence of another person named in the Management Structure.

102. You have used your self rescuer to reach the CABA supply. Can your self rescuer be used again? YES / NO

It is unlikely that someone who has not been trained will know the answer. This type of question can also be used to see how the group feels about a controversial or misunderstood topic.

It can be useful in a pre-test so that content can be matched to the needs of the group.

Paired choices

Even with questions 100 to 102 a candidate who guesses has a 50-50 chance of getting it right. To prevent guessing, some designers give one point for a correct answer and lose half a point for an incorrect one. If the question is not attempted there are no points gained or lost.

It is even better to use a series of paired choice questions together, as in this example:

103. Which vehicle has right of way in each of these cases:

Circle the correct option in each case

a) *A transport vehicle carrying workers outbye at the end of shift meets an LHD towing a drivehead.*
   Transport
   LHD
b) *A transport vehicle carrying workers inbye at start of shift meets a loader travelling to pit bottom.*
   Loader
   Transporter
c) *An LHD towing a trailer meets an official travelling in a Transporter*
   LHD
   Transporter
d) *A loader travelling outbye meets a transport travelling inbye*
   Transporter
   Loader
e) *A grader is grading the road and a transport vehicle needs to pass*
   Grader
   Transporter

The answers to these questions will depend on local rules, but when you set up the list make sure that all the correct answers are not in the same column or in the left then the right then the left then the right.

These questions have been worded to test more than the transport rules. LHD and loader are basically the same. This may also be another way of testing a new person's knowledge of jargon.

104. Who has the responsibility under the legislation in these cases?

GM is the General Manager, MM is the Mine Manager, OCE is the Open Cut Examiner and ERZ is the ERZ Controller.

While both options may perform the duty at some mines, this question is to assess your understanding of who has the duty under the legislation.

   a) *To train coal mine workers so that they are competent to perform their duties*
      GM   OCE
   b) *To provide for regular monitoring and assessment of the working environment, work procedures, equipment, and installations at the mine*
      GM   ERZ
   c) *To provide for appropriate inspection of each workplace at the mine including, where necessary, pre-shift inspections*
      GM   ERZ
   d) *Be involved in developing and testing the emergency management procedures*
      GM   OCE
   e) *To be involved in auditing the documentation for the emergency management procedures*
      GM   ERZ
   f) *To control the highwall mining activity while an abnormal circumstances declaration is in force*
      ERZ   MM

g) *To review the principal hazard management plans and standard operating procedures in consultation with coal mine workers*
    GM   ERZ
h) *To authorise a person to be issued with an explosive powered tool or cartridge*
    MM   ERZ
i) *To ensure the area from which the sample was taken is re-treated with stonedust, if an analysis of a dust sample shows the dust does not comply with the incombustible material content*
    MM   ERZ
j) *Read the record of the latest regular periodic inspection findings of an ERZ and acknowledge this in writing on the record.*
    ERZ   MM

Knowing who has what responsibility is an important part of the legislation.

Level of assessment

In this set I have asked the same basic question, but put it in a different way for operators, supervisors and managers. This might be a useful tool to check understanding of a new policy. I used it in an investigation following an accident, where the person overtaken clearly had a different understanding of the rules to the person who was being overtaken. When the whole workforce was tested there was clearly a need for clarification of the procedure and all were retrained.

105. For Managers

Managers are people who give directions that affect the safety and health of workers, but who are not in the working area for a major part of their working day. They make strategic or tactical decisions rather than day to day operational ones. Their answers should reflect their responsibilities.

a) *While you are explaining a company policy to a crew, one of the employees says that there are radio black spots in their circuit. What would you do?*
b) *While you are at the main mine office you notice that a new Mine Record Entry is on display. You have not seen it before, and when you read it, you believe that it may affect the way your people work. Because they do not start at the main site, they are not likely to see it. What steps would you take?*
c) *What steps would you take before a new type of truck is introduced to the mine? This type of truck is in common use at other mine sites, and some of your employees may be familiar with it, but it is likely that most are not.*
d) *There is a severe lightning storm approaching the mine site. How would you estimate its distance from your location? If you estimate that storm is about 25 km away, what steps would you take?*
e) *What would you look for when conducting an investigation following an incident where a truck has run into a windrow towards the end of night shift on the last day of a rotation?*

106. For Supervisors

Supervisors are people who work in the mine and give directions that affect the safety and health of coal mine workers for a major part of their working day. Trainers and Assessors should also do this assessment before they do the operator one.

a) *While you are explaining a JSEA to a crew, one of the employees says that there are radio black spots in the circuit. What would you do?*
b) *While you are at the main mine office you notice that a new Mine Record Entry is on display. You have not seen it before, and when you read it you believe that it may affect the way your people work. Because they do not start at the main site they are not likely to see it. What steps would you take?*
c) *An operator tells you that he has not driven the type of truck he has been assigned to before. He is authorised to operate all the other trucks at the site. What would you do?*

d) *There is a severe lightning storm approaching the mine site. How would you estimate its distance from your location? If you estimate that storm is about 25 km away, what steps would you take?*
e) *An employee tells you that she is feeling tired. She has had a bad week and hasn't slept well. What would you do?*

107. For Operators

Operators are people who are authorised or under minimal supervision under the training scheme. Trainers and assessors should do the operator assessment after they have completed the supervisor one.

There may be more than one right answer to some questions. Tick all the things that you think are right.

a) *There are radio black spots in your circuit. What would you do?*
   i. Stop work
   ii. Change to another radio channel
   iii. Go to a place where the radio is working and call the supervisor
   iv. Stop any other vehicles that are coming into the area
   v. Continue working as long as the radio works most of the time

b) *You think you may have bent a ladder on your machine. You brushed against a windrow in a tight spot. What would you do?*
   i. Get down and check it
   ii. Call up the supervisor on the radio
   iii. Isolate the machine
   iv. Tag the machine out of service
   v. Make a report in the shift log

c) *You need to overtake a grader that is working on the haul road. You call up on the radio and do not get a reply. Can you pass the machine?*
   i. No. Overtaking is banned unless I have permission from the driver of the other vehicle

    ii. Yes. The grader driver does not have to reply if the implements are engaged
    iii. No, if I am driving a heavy vehicle
    iv. Yes, if I am driving a light vehicle

d) A new type of truck is in the circuit. You have been authorised to operate all the other types of trucks at the mine. What must you do before you operate the new truck?
    i. Tell the supervisor and follow instructions
    ii. Ask a trainer assessor to check me out on the truck
    iii. Only operate under close supervision until I have been assessed
    iv. Operate under minimal supervision until I feel confident
    v. Not operate the machine until I have an authorisation signed by the General Manager or a delegate.

e) There is a lightning storm getting very close. What would you do?
    i. Continue working. The safest place in a storm is in a heavy vehicle
    ii. Wait until it starts to rain, then pull up if the roads become greasy
    iii. Pull up in a safe place and stay in the truck
    iv. Pull up in a safe place and get as far away from the truck as possible
    v. Call up the supervisor and follow instructions
    vi. Tip my load and go back to the go line

f) You are starting to yawn and are feeling a bit tired. What would you do?

Bingo cards

Each person is given a card with different contents. Some terms may be duplicated, and critical items may be included on all cards.

> Your assessor will go with you on a walk underground. Tell the assessor when you see each of the things on this Bingo Card

Sign for secondary escapeway	Lifeline	CABA station
Sign for primary escapeway	Rib spall	Emergency button on telephone
Explosion Barrier	Fire depot	Swilly
Jet nozzle	Fire hydrant	Deputy Station
Fog nozzle	Guttering	First Aid station
Compressed air line	Water line	Pump out line

This is a good test of familiarity with local terms as well as observation skills.

Practical Demonstrations

While many of the earlier questions have dealt with application as well as recall and understanding, an assessment can also include specifically practical questions.

The first are practical observations of following a procedure. Whether the candidate has a copy of the procedure to follow will depend on normal practice in the workplace. If the trained employee is expected to remember the procedure, do not provide one. If the task is performed regularly, the assessment may include locating the procedure and following it.

108. Collect a gas detector to use with a diesel vehicle.

    a) Book out detector

b) *Test detector on surface (list relevant steps in test that are local practice)*
c) *Carry detector carefully*
d) *Place detector in suitable position on vehicle.*

109. Show how you would check your lamp before taking it underground at start of shift.

a) *Take the assigned light.*
b) *Is battery charged*
c) *Is battery leaking*
d) *Is battery damaged?*
e) *Is high beam working*
f) *Is low beam working*

When candidate checks low beam, tell them to continue as though the low beam bulb is not working.

g) *Is glass damaged*
h) *Is glass retaining ring damaged*
i) *Select spare lamp from appropriate supply*
j) *Check the condition of the spare lamp battery, glass and globes as above (parts b to h)*
k) *Fill in lamp issue register (actually do this on a specimen page, not just tell how it is done.)*
l) *Tag damaged lamp. (Do this on an actual tag, not just tell how it is done.)*

Other practical assessment questions

As well as the various written tests described here, you can also ask candidates to

- Mark items on a plan
- Draw a sketch, or
- Label a diagram

110. Mark items on a plan

Most of the information about the place is already shown, but the candidate adds the required features. A list of symbols to be used should be included.

Other examples where marking on a plan could be used include:

- Traffic sign locations
- Fire equipment installation
- Ventilation control locations in a building

111. Label a diagram

Use a diagram with all the items shown, but without labels for assessing knowledge on

- Component parts or controls layout on any item
- Traffic flow near a pedestrian area
- Location of items in a supermarket or warehouse
- Locations of restricted items in a warehouse.

112. Draw a sketch

Unless you are assessing artistic ability, keep requests for sketches to ones that can be completed with a few boxes, circles or lines, such as relative positions of cars in an accident, or suitable locations for fragile or high use parts in a warehouse.

Observation Checklist

The mining example shown below has two levels of observation – the individual job steps, such as "pick up the remote control" and the actions within each step, such as the way it is carried and its on/off status.

You can develop a similar checklist for any activity in your field of work, in conjunction with people who do the job well and with supervisor to make sure their expectation is met.

113. Continuous Miner Operation

The candidate can be observed starting the miner at start of shift or after a delay, cut and load at least two bolting cycles and shut down at the end of shift or for a break in production. This may mean that the assessor must observe the operator three times to see start up, tramming and shut down.

Sample Only – Not to be used as standard assessment. This is the result of one risk assessment involving competent people at one mine. With a broad cross section of your work force you can do better

Task	Standard
Pick up remote control	Ready for use tag attached
	Lid secure, case straps, switches in good condition
	No loose parts – shake test
	Carry in OFF position with Mechanical guard over switch.
Take remote to section	Carry in OFF position with mechanical guard over switch
	Not to be taken past crib room if another unit on this frequency inbye
Preparation	wearing PPE
	High visibility clothing
	No loose clothing
	Safety glasses
Coordination	Discuss driveage plan with
	ERZ Controller

Task	Standard
	Roof bolters
	Shuttle car drivers
Condition of workplace	Inspect supports set on previous shift
	Check miner is on line and level
	Condition of roof and sides
	Ventilation and gas
Access and exit	3 point contact
Pre start checks	Complete transmitter (remote) pre-use checklist
	Walk around inspection
	Remove slip / trip hazards from standing and working area
Cutting	Position miner on centre
	Loader plate on floor
	Ventilation is up to face
	Water sprays on
	Tail clear of coal in car
	Cutting direction roof to floor
	Avoid cutting roof
Standing position	Stand outside of NO STANDING zone.
	Can see miner from standing position
	Can see other workers from position
	Stops miner when changes position
	Tells shuttle car driver when changing position
If cutting breakaway may stand in NO STANDING zone after safety assessment	
Flit or tram miner at least 20 metres	Inspect route before tramming (visual inspection for short distance – walk route if around corners.)
	Warn other people nearby that miner is going to move
	Stand outside of NO STANDING zones

Task	Standard
	Stop miner if other people come into CONTROL ZONE
	Watch cable. Coordinate with cable handlers
Shut down after use	Miner parked 5 m outbye last support
	Head, shovel and boom lowered
	Miner control from RADIO to OFF
	On board isolator OFF
	Remote taken to crib room and left as spare or taken to surface if spare in section.

Log books

Log books serve two purposes:

- To show that certain tasks have been done,
- To identify areas where the work was done for later inspection.

114. Development machine log book review

    a) Assessor to inspect roadway driven previously by candidate for:
        i. Support spacing
        ii. Driven on line and level
        iii. Holes in roof or floor
        iv. Width of the roadway

    b) Candidate to provide log book record of these tasks:
        i. Set up the miner at start of shift
        ii. Shut down the miner at end of shift
        iii. Drive straight heading
        iv. Drive breakaway
        v. Hole into standing place
        vi. Flit the miner at least 50 metres and around corner

115. Supplies loader log book review

    a) Assessor to inspect areas where supplies placed previously by candidate for:
        i. General tidiness
        ii. Suitable location – accessible but out of the way
        iii. Assessor to inspect area where candidate has cleaned road
        iv. Cables and hoses tied up out of way
        v. Road cleaning standard

    b) Candidate to provide log book record of these tasks:
        i. Use jib, forks, bucket
        ii. Change between implements – e.g.: jib to forks OR forks to bucket OR bucket to jib

  iii. Clean road with bucket
  iv. Carry supplies on fork
  v. Relocate item with jib ... etc to suit local use of equipment

Situational Awareness

There is a common element in many competencies:

- Obtain, interpret and clarify/confirm work requirements before proceeding.

or

- Access, interpret and apply environmental data required to complete the allocated work.

An effective way to assess this practically is with these questions

116. Tell me about two things that were mentioned at the start of shift meeting today

117. Can you tell me what the current reading is for the:

 a) Gas or air readings for a monitored point underground
 b) The barometer
 c) Current (Amps) reading on an electric motor
 d) RPM on a vehicle tachometer

Watch the person get the necessary information, then follow up with question – how does this affect the job you are going to do?

118. Can you get me a copy of a nominated procedure?

Watch the person retrieve it from the appropriate place.

www.ingramcontent.com/pod-product-compliance
Lightning Source LLC
Chambersburg PA
CBHW020448220526
45464CB00002B/914